The 5 Elements of the
Highly Effective Debt Collector

The 5 Elements of the
Highly Effective Debt Collector

How to become a
Top Performing Debt Collector
In Less than 30 Days!!!

The Powerful Training System for Developing
Efficient, Effective & Top Performing Debt Collectors

TIMOTHY J. DAYE

IUNIVERSE, INC.
BLOOMINGTON

The 5 Elements of the Highly Effective Debt Collector
How to become a Top Performing Debt Collector In Less than 30 Days!!! The Powerful
Training System for Developing Efficient, Effective & Top Performing Debt Collectors

First Edition: 2011

iUniverse books may be ordered through booksellers or by contacting:

iUniverse
1663 Liberty Drive
Bloomington, IN 47403
www.iuniverse.com
1-800-Authors (1-800-288-4677)

This publication is designed to provide accurate and authoritative information in regard to the subject matter covered. It is sold with the understanding that the publisher is not engaged in rendering legal, accounting or other professional service. If legal advice or other expert assistance is required, the services of a competent professional person should be sought.

This production is not a substitute for legal advice

Because of the dynamic nature of the Internet, any web addresses or links contained in this book may have changed since publication and may no longer be valid. The views expressed in this work are solely those of the author and do not necessarily reflect the views of the publisher, and the publisher hereby disclaims any responsibility for them.

Any people depicted in stock imagery provided by Thinkstock are models, and such images are being used for illustrative purposes only.
Certain stock imagery © Thinkstock.

ISBN: 978-1-4620-3329-4 (sc)
ISBN: 978-1-4620-3330-0 (ebk)

Printed in the United States of America

iUniverse rev. date: 07/08/2011

I would like to give a special thanks to CEO Tommy Moore, COO Blaise Rodon, Diane Reinari, Alisha Campbell, Toni Mckinney, Helena Barber and all my dear friends at First Investors. I am truly graceful for the opportunity to have worked for this great organization. This dynamic company gave me the discipline and direction I needed to take my ability to the next level. For this I will be forever indebted.

I would also like to give an individual salute to collection manager Tungi Davis. Thanks for recognizing my talent and taking a special interest in my early development; also for pushing me to understand that for my talent level, simply being number one was not enough.

Contents

Fair Debt Collection Practices Act

- Contacting the debtor 1
- Mailed correspondences to the debtor 2
- Contact with a Third Party..2
- Debtor's remedies if provisions are violated.......................................2

Different Types of Debt

- Secured loans..3
- Unsecured loans 3
- Taxes 3

Creditor's Remedies for Unpaid Debt

- Wage Attachment..4
- Repossession..4

Bankruptcy

- Chapter 7 5
- Chapter 13 5

Differences Between First Party & Third Party Collections

- First Party..6
- Third Party..6

Introduction

The 5 Elements of The Highly Effective Debt Collector

Language is King

Element #1: Voicemail Message Leaving

- The Collector's Workday 11
- "Voicemail Messages" The Productivity that Drives Effectiveness 12
- The method behind my success 13
- Understanding what makes a quality voicemail message 14
- The sound of your voice 14
- Diction & Language 14
- Expanding your Vocabulary 15
- Creativity 15
- Multiple Messages, Tone, & Consistency 16

Element #2: The Talk-Off

- Communicate, Negotiate, Capitalize 18
- The Basic Structure of an Effective Talk-Off 19
- Taking Control of a Conversation 19
- The First Step to Taking Control "Reposition" 20
- Establishing Full Control 20
- Disclose the reason for the call, but "DON'T GO FOR THE MONEY" 21
- Cue the debtor to speak 22
- Have the debtor make a simple "yes or no" decision 22
- The Close . . . "Going for the money" 23
- Build rapport but stay firm 23
- Getting the bank information 24
- Redirecting 24
- If the debtor doesn't have a bank account 25
- Why give 24-hours to purchase a prepaid if the debtor does not have the money today? 26
- Avoid setting the debtor up for failure 26

Element #3: Rebuttals

- Never let the debtor escalate the call 27
- Feel, Felt, Found 28
- This debt does not belong to me 28
- I paid this debt off 29
- The take away close 30

Element #4: The Reference Relay

- The concept of the Reference Relay...31
- Create solid third party messages...32
- The initial third party message..32
- Don't sound like a collector..33
- Be Pleasant..33
- The open for an Effective Reference Relay.......................................34
- Avoid disclosing to a spouse..34

Element #5: File Management

- Defining File Management..36
- Effectiveness..37
- Numbers hiding the numbers...38
- The limitation of collections software..38
- Vagueness of status codes..39
- The File Management Tracker...40
- How to use the File Management Tracker.......................................40
- Messages side of the tracker..40
- Debtor Contact side of the tracker...42
- Document messages not calls...42
- No double entries..43
- Never place third party's names on track.......................................43

Exhibit A

- File Management Tracker...45

Exhibit B

- File Management Tracker...46

Conclusion

Debt Terms

- A-Z..49

Reference

Fair Debt Collection Practices Act

The **Fair Debt Collection Practices Act** (**FDCPA**), is a United States statute added in 1978 as Title VIII of the Consumer Credit Protection Act. The purpose of the Act was to set forth specifics as to how persons collecting a debt may behave toward individuals owing a debt and promote fair debt collection. The Act also provides consumers with an avenue for disputing and obtaining validation of debt information in order to ensure the information's accuracy. In essence it creates guidelines under which debt collectors may conduct business, defines rights of consumers involved with debt collectors, and prescribes penalties and remedies for violations of the Act. These sections apply not only to actual collection agencies, but people acting as debt collectors.

Contacting the debtor

Debtors may not be contacted at unusual or inconvenient times (before 8 a.m. and after 9 p.m.) or at work if the debtor is not permitted to accept such calls at their work place. A collector may not call repeatedly nor call without identifying who they are. A collector may not cause a debtor to be responsible for the cost of a call, such as calling collect. A collector may not identify him/herself as being a part of law enforcement or as an attorney. A collector may not harass, oppress, or abuse the debtor. A collector may not use or threaten to use violence or harm to the debtor or anyone connected to the debtor, or damage a debtor's reputation. If the debtor has an attorney, a collector must speak with that attorney and not the debtor, unless the debtor gives the collector permission. (FDCPA, Sec. 1692(c) and (d).)

A collector may not use obscene language. A debtor's name may not be published on a deadbeat list. If you contact a debtor and if he/she instructs you not to call them again you must adhere to this request, and you may only notify the debtor by mail as to the status of their account. (FDCPA, Sec. 1692(c) through (f).)

A collector cannot deceive a debtor as to the amount of debt, nor can threaten to take action against the debtor that the creditor and/or agency do not intend to take. A collector cannot use unfair or outrageous attempts to collect a debt; such as adding interest or fees not part of the original debt, asking for a postdated check by threatening the debtor with criminal action, accepting a check that is more than five days postdated unless a collector notifies the debtor three to ten days before cashing the check. A collector may not deposit a postdated check before the date assigned. (FDCPA, Sec. 1692(f).)

Mailed correspondences to the debtor

When sending mailed correspondences to a debtor, it must not appear to be or resemble court documents or correspondences from a government agency or from an attorney. The envelope used must be plain and cannot indicate anywhere on it that it is in reference to the collection of a debt or that it is from a collection agency. (FDCPA, Sec. 1692(e).)

Contact with a Third Party

As a collector you must give your name when contacting a third party (persons other than the individual that owes the debt). A collector must state that he/she is confirming or correcting residential or employment information for the debtor. If asked, a collector may give the agency that he/she works for, however a collector may not at any point discuss the debt with the third party. A collector may not call a third party more than once unless the collector received incorrect or incomplete information or unless the third party gives permission. (FDCPA, Sec. 16929(b).)

Debtor's remedies if provisions are violated

Debtors may send a letter to their state attorney general detailing the violation. They may also send a letter to the Federal Trade Commission in their region.

The debtor may also bring the case to small claims court for punitive damages and can be rewarded up to $1000.00. (FDCPA, Sec. 1692(k).)

__Different Types of Debt__

Secured loans

Secured loans are loans where an individual borrows money from a creditor to buy a certain item and give the creditor a security interest or collateral in the item. When an individual for example takes out a car loan, he/she gives the creditor the right to take (repossess) the car if he/she does not pay the loan. A Mortgage is a type of secured loan.

Unsecured loans

An unsecured loan occurs when creditors lend an individual money and the creditors, do not have a security interest in anything the person owns. An example of an unsecured loan is a credit card. However, a credit card that is secured through an individual's bank account is considered a secured loan, because the creditor can seize the debtor's bank account if the debt is not paid. A Student loan is a form of an unsecured loan.

Taxes

Taxes are an amount owed to the state or federal government.

Creditor's Remedies for Unpaid Debt

In the case a debtor does not pay a debt, there are several legal avenues a creditor can pursue.

Wage Attachment

Creditors have the right to look to a debtor's wages as a means to seek repayment for a debt owed and can have the debtor's employer pay the creditor or agency directly.

There are two ways to attach wages **wage garnishment** and **wage assignment**.

A **wage garnishment** occurs when a court enters a judgment against the debtor and the creditor is allowed to take out a portion of the debtor's wages. (Each states law varies on amount, or if wage garnishment is allowed). The debtor must be served papers and a court must hear the debtor's case before a wage garnishment. However, if the debtor ignores court papers, a court can order the judgment without the debtor's consent and/or knowledge.

A **wage assignment** occurs when a debtor agrees to have a portion of his/her wages sent directly to the creditor. This method can never occur without the debtor's consent or knowledge.

Repossession

Repossession occurs when a creditor has a security interest or collateral in an item an individual purchases and the loan taken to purchase the item goes into default. The creditor has the right to regain possession of the item because the debtor did not pay. If an item, for example a vehicle, is repossessed, the debtor will still owe the remainder of the loan balance and any cost and/or fees associated the repossession process. **Foreclosure** is a legal form of repossession for real estate

Bankruptcy

Bankruptcy is a procedure that a debtor can go through in federal bankruptcy court that allows them to discharge all or part of their debt. When the debtor files a petition with the court declaring he/she is bankrupt, all of the debtor's creditors (by law) must stop any collection activity. This is referred to as an **automatic stay**, where by the creditor cannot repossess a debtor's vehicle, garnish wages, or call about a debt owed. In this process, a trustee is appointed and will be in charge of dividing the debtor's asset among the creditors.

Chapter 7

A Chapter 7 bankruptcy allows the debtor to discharge all of his/her debt; this is referred to as **liquidation.** In this process the trustee legally takes possession of all assets that are not exempt under state or federal law and liquidates (sell) the items for cash to pay the debtor's creditors. Debts that cannot be discharged are alimony, child support, taxes, and student loans.

Chapter 13

A Chapter 13 bankruptcy, referred to as **reorganization**, allows the debtor to keep most assets. However, a three to five year payment plan is arranged where full or partial payment of the debt owed will be paid. Taxes are included in a 13 chapter.

Differences Between First Party
& Third Party Collections

In pursuit of employment as a debt collector, you will have to understand on what terms the company or agency will be representing the debt being collected. The laws surrounding the debt collecting practice will differ depending upon how the company or agency represents the debt in question.

First Party

Collection agencies can represent a debt in one of two ways, as a first party or a third party, (second party is the debtor). First party agencies are subsidiaries or division of the original company the debt is owed. These agencies are referred to as First party because the company owns the debt, and/or the "first party" to contract. Because these agencies are part of the original contract, first party agencies are not subject to the FDCPA, however most first party agencies try to maintain a constructive relationship with the debtor. These agencies are involved early in the collection process before the debt is written off as uncollectible.

Third Party

A third party collection agency is a company that was not part of the original contract. The first party (the creditor) assigns accounts to a third party agency on a contingency basis, meaning that the third party agency will receive a percentage of the debt that is successfully collected. These agencies are governed by the (FDCPA).

Introduction

The 5 Elements of The Highly Effective Debt Collector

"The illiterate of the 21ˢᵗ Century will not be those who cannot read and write, but those who cannot learn, unlearn, and relearn."
Alvin Toffler

Through out my career in the collection industry as a top producing collector, collections manager, and trainer, I have found that far too many collectors are underdeveloped. There are multiple reasons for this lack of development; nonetheless the root cause and the most prevailing of all would be that the industry has not found the fine line between customer service training and sales training techniques to satisfy the collections training practice. As a result of the industry's inability to create an effective training model that lay between these two disciplines, collectors are given short (FDCPA) compliance training sessions on what not to do or say. For example, a new hire will go through collections training given brief sessions of the laws governing the industry and the penalties for violating provisions, but never given any sound communication concepts, effective negotiating techniques nor file management principles that would build a solid foundation for a would be collector. One would think; the goal for any industry or organization would be to develop new talent effectively as possible to put an individual in a situation that is more likely to have them succeed, yet this is far from the case. Collectors are often introduced to the collections floor with little sense of direction, and left to figure out how to become effective on their own. This I would argue is the primary reason for the explosion of abusive tactics used in the industry, as well as the lack of professionalism associated with the debt collections practice.

The truth is, the industry has not produced clearly defined fundamental concepts for collectors to become professionals. As a matter of fact, debt collections is the only profession (business or recreation) where universal fundamental concepts does not exist. A basketball coach for example can watch a basketball game, and no matter the talent level of the team or individual player could point out specific areas and determine why the team or individual is performing at a high level or under achieving based on universal fundamental concepts of the game of basketball. This is true for any profession, from high profile practices such as law, engineering, or accounting, to jobs as domestic as mopping a floor or lawn care; there are certain core concepts that have to be taught and understood to ensure the job is done as effectively and efficiently as possible. As a consequence of the absence of such fundamental principles required to effectively train and develop debt collectors, training divisions are the weakest area in any agency; and as a result, collection agencies across the country lose millions of dollars annually in the form of mishandled accounts, mismanaged files, and extremely high turnover rates. For instance, I recall as a collector early in my career attending a training class of 14 people. Frankly, this company's training division was a joke. The training was a four-day process that consisted of the trainer explaining how much money a person could make if we could be effective, training on how to operate the collections software, the distributing of scripted voicemail messages that basically said, "*please don't call me back*" along with a brief (FDCPA) training session followed by a (FDCPA) multiple-choice test to confirm that the trainer at least discussed the topic. Needless to say, after a month of working on the phones only four of the training class remained. This type of sink or swim model is very common in the world of collections; **it's either you ARE or ARE NOT an effective collector**. This is true because there are no core fundamentals to determine the reason(s) why a collector is excelling or **more importantly, why a collector may not be producing at a desired level**. To clarify this point as it pertains to the under performing collector, I offer this analogy. Consider for a moment, if you were to wake up on a given morning, jump in your car for your daily commute, and as luck would have it your vehicle would not start. Reluctantly, you have the unit towed to an auto repair shop. The mechanic, following his diagnoses of your vehicle tells you, "*Well . . . Maim/Sir, it looks like the problem is your car won't start*". I'm sure after receiving this news, you would (more than likely) be upset, and have a few choice words for this brilliant mechanic. The reason you would be so upset and/or disappointed in the mechanic's analysis is simple, **you understand the car not starting is not the problem**. The car not starting is the result of some other underlying problem i.e. dead battery, bad starter, or bad alternator etc. The same can be said for a collector that is under producing. The problem isn't the collector cannot produce; the collector not being able to produce at a desired level is the result of some underlying issue(s). After years as a top collector, as well as training and developing top performers, I have assembled what are the five fundamental areas that are required to effectively train, and develop any person attempting to collect a debt. These five core areas are also at the center of revealing and repairing any performance issue(s) a debt collector may experience. The 5 elements are as follows:

1. **Voicemail Message Leaving**: The productivity that drives effectiveness. The systematic approach to message leaving.
2. **Talk-Off:** Communicate, Negotiate, and Capitalize (CNC). How to use persuasive language and position to convince debtors to pay.

3. **<u>Rebuttals:</u>** How to use effective sale techniques to overcome the most common debtor objections.
4. **<u>Reference Relay</u>:** How to consistently persuade third parties to help you locate and make contact with the debtor.
5. **<u>File Management</u>:** How to properly manage a collections file to enhance efficiency and reveal important information about a collector's effectiveness.

Understanding how each area works together will show exactly how a deficiency in one specific area can tremendously reduce a collector's earning potential as well as explain how the mastery of each will transform an individual into a concept that I created called **The Complete Collector**. We describe **The Complete Collector** as a skilled verbal communicator, highly effective negotiator, trained and developed in the five core fundamental areas of consumer debt collections.

The 5 Elements of the Highly Effective Debt Collector is the first of a series of books intended to confront many misconceptions, inefficiencies, and the most common mistakes made not only by the individual collector; but also issues plaguing collection agency operations as a whole. However, this book was created to develop and enhance effectiveness of the individual collector and is designed to ensure that no matter an individual's talent level, years in the industry, or position held in a collections agency, the end user will understand clearly and be enriched by the experience. More specifically, it will introduce core fundamental concepts, sound principles of engagement, and a system of file management that if followed and executed properly will more than double a collector's efficiency and effectiveness in less than 30 days. However, before we get into the 5 elements, first we must start with the importance of **"using effective language."**

Language is King

The primary objective of a debt collector would be to use language to persuade a debtor to surrender his/her money, which is no different than a salesman. However, the distinction between a debtor and a sales prospect is a debtor will not receive a new service or a shiny new toy for forking over his/her hard earned cash. The reward for paying a debt is built around the debtor avoiding some type of consequence. Therefore, effectively communicating the possible consequences if a debt is not paid will play a large factor in determining how successful an individual will be collecting a debt. Using proper language, diction, transition words and phrases when explaining what could potentially happen if a debt is not paid creates a degree of creditability that is essential when communicating and/or negotiating via the telephone. For instance, as a collector I would usually reach my monthly goal first, sometimes weeks before my counterparts and I was often asked how I did it or what I was saying to convince debtors to pay in such a timely fashion. I would tell them *"I'm not a collector"* . . . *"I'm a creditability builder"* . . . *"First you must sound credible and the money will follow"*. As a debt collector it must be understood, when engaging with a debtor, creditability is built on the front-end, and money is collected on the backend. Frankly speaking, people will not give their money or provide personal-banking information to anyone that does not sound credible. "**It's not what you say . . . it's how you say it**" this adage is at the very core of communicating, who you are, who you are representing, why you are calling, and above all, how the situation can be handled without recourse. Effectively communicating and using the proper language and diction creates power. Power, not in the sense of brut force, though power as defined by Webster is the "possession of controlling influence", which language will create if used properly.

Element #1:
<u>Voicemail Message Leaving</u>

The proper place to start is where the collecting process begins for a collector, **voicemail message leaving**. Voicemail message leaving has been and will continue to be a touchy area, since there are (**FDCPA**) provisions restricting what can or cannot be said when leaving a voicemail message. And the fact that voice messages are recorded, if provision(s) are violated, it's somewhat difficult to defend yourself or the company against such hard evidence. Nonetheless, voicemail message leaving is an extremely crucial area to master within the 5 elements, because your initial success will not be determined on how well you negotiate or communicate; as your negotiating and/or communicating talent means very little if the ability cannot be displayed. Your initial success will first come down to how effective and efficient you are at persuading debtors to return your calls, which puts you in position to use your communication and/or negotiating talent. This is a notion that is often taken for granted on collection floors across the country, and the primary reason why most new comers to the collection industry fail within the first 60 to 90 days of their employment with an agency_ it's the inability to consistently and effectively make contact. However, I will share with you a set of concepts, principles, and tactics that will help you leap this hurtle and give you a firm grasp of how to initially approach your career as a collector in the infant stages of your development. Understanding the following ideals will significantly reduce your learning curve and set you on the proper path to being a top performer.

The Collector's Workday

The first step on the pathway to becoming a top performer you must understand how to approach your workday. Most individuals in or outside of the industry believe the most important portion of a collector's workday would be setting up payment arrangements. Although setting up payment arrangements is the ultimate goal for a collector, it is the smallest portion of what a collector will do on a daily basis, and is the direct result of the largest and most important part of a collector's daily work activity. To explain this point say for example, a collector working three-year-old credit card debt was somehow able to set up ten new payment arrangements in one given workday, which is unrealistic for debt that is three years old or older. For a seasoned collector, it would take between ten to fifteen minutes of talk time to deliver a

Talk-off, negotiate the debt, and set up arrangements for each of the ten new promises, which if we were to use simple math, would only constitute twenty percent of the collector's daily work activity. Considering this information, it should be obvious that even if a collector was able to produce at an insanely high level, the majority of his/her workday will be spent in an attempt to locate and make contact with debtors. This extremely important process of locating debtors will be done one of two ways; **directly**, (calling possible direct phone numbers provided on the debtor's account such as home or cellular phone number) or **indirectly**, referred to as **skip tracing** (a process of finding direct or indirect phone numbers that are not found on the debtor's file such as phone numbers for relatives or close associates). The reason I want to make this point abundantly clear is that most beginners when introduced to the collections floor will make the mistake of first devising a plan of attack for the smallest portion of their workday rather than the largest. To have immediate success in the infant stages of your career as a debt collector you must understand that, **although what to do or say once a debtor is on the phone is the most vital part of a collector producing at a high level; however for the beginner your initial focus should be two part: First, to create a system that effectively and efficiently locates debtors. Second, to develop language that consistently convinces debtors to return your calls, as this is the activity that will ultimately keep you in a position to capitalize throughout your career.**

"Voicemail Messages" The Productivity that Drives Effectiveness

Productivity is defined as the measure of output from a production process, per unit of input. In the collection industry productivity is measured by the number of phone numbers dialed by a specific collector for a given day, week, or month, (the number of calls concept); and as a collector at any agency in the country there will be immense pressure for you to meet a daily calls quota. The **number of calls concept** says there is a direct correlation between the number of calls a collector dials and how many debtors a collector will potentially make contact with, (the law of large numbers). Although this concept holds true in the sales profession, for the collections practice this concept is limited. The reason this method is not truly effective for the collector is that it does not take into account one extremely important variable; **it does not take into account if the collector left a voicemail message**. To illustrate this limitation, say for example two collectors, Collector A and Collector B used the exact language, tone, and delivery for each voicemail message left during a given day. At the end of the day, Collector A dialed 60 phone numbers and left 40 voicemail messages and Collector B dialed 100 phone numbers and only leaves 20 voicemail messages. With all things being equal except number of phone numbers dialed, and number of messages left, it stands to reason that Collector A will yield the most success. This is true because Collector A delivered twice the number of requests for a return call; and the fact that Collector B dialed twice as many phone numbers means very little, other than Collector B wasted a lot of valuable time.

What's more, the limitations of this concept push collectors to the point of **"fudging calls"**. **Call Fudging** is a trick collectors use to please management and avoid reprimand, by dialing the same phone numbers over and over to make it appear as though they were being productive. As a consequence of using this deception, the collector will not be working to generate money, but simply dialing phone numbers to hit a calls quota. For instance, I remember working for a third party agency collecting credit card debt. I was the top collector in the office and would hit my monthly goal eight to ten days before my peers; though I usually made the least amount of calls. Management would be baffled as to how I could accomplish this with so few calls, but would never look for the true reason for my high level of success. Oddly enough, irregardless of my high performance and effectiveness with so few calls, in comparison to my colleague's low performance and ineffectiveness whom met or surpassed their calls quota (with obvious call fudging), I would be reprimanded. This was one of the toughest things I ever had to deal with in my entire career. Imagine, instead of management searching for the reasons why my peers were under performing and costing the company time and money; I would be reprimanded for over performing and saving the company time and money. In response to this oxymoron, management would tell me I was smarter or more talented than my peers and that, *"I shouldn't try to take advantage of the system"*. When in fact, **the system** was not taking full advantage of me, and what I had to offer.

Despite the obvious disadvantages and limitations to the number of calls concept, collection agencies love to see high call volumes and will go to extremes just to see some "pie in the sky" high number. One example of an extreme measure taken by agencies to boost call volumes is implementing a dialer system. A Dialer is a system an agency will use that automatically dials phone numbers for the collector. These systems are used solely to crank up call volumes, yet does nothing to enhance effectiveness. As a matter of fact, to the surprise of most collections executive management teams after implementing such a system see very little difference or maybe even a decline in the agency's bottom line, even though the agency's call volume may have doubled. I want to be clear; I am not suggesting that the number of calls a collector dials is not important, because it will play a role in a collector's overall productivity. This is more of an attempt to explain how the number of calls a collector dials will not be the force that will drive his or her effectiveness. **The first realization that started my high level of success was understanding that the productivity that drove my effectiveness rested on the amount of quality and consistent voicemail messages I left in a given day, week, or month that were connected to the debtor, be it direct or indirect.**

The method behind my success

There were numerous reasons I performed at a much higher level than my counterparts. However, once I understood that leaving more messages was the productivity that drove my effectiveness, I made three changes. First, I switched my goal from dialing more numbers to leaving more messages. Second, I concentrated on the quality of my messages and lastly I developed a system that ensured my messages were delivered consistently.

Understanding what makes a quality voicemail message

We describe a quality voicemail message as using proper **sound of voice, tone, diction**, and **language** when delivering a voicemail message. Collectors are often puzzled, as to why they cannot persuade more debtors to return their call, after leaving numerous messages. The truth is they are deficient in one or all of these following areas.

The sound of your voice

The reason why some singers are more successful than others isn't because of the lyrics of the song or melody, although it may help. The largest part of their success is determined by the sound of the singer's voice. The voice is what catches and holds the attention of the audience. When leaving a voicemail message this is no different; it's the voice of the message leaver that will catch the individual's attention. One of the funniest things to have happen when working on a phone, is to have a someone return your call, only to confess that the reason he/she called back was the sound of your voice. Unfortunately, you have or don't have a strong phone voice, this is a gift from up above and there is very little you can do to change it. If this could be changed, we would all sound like Celine Dion. If you don't have a great phone voice don't fret, your career as a collector isn't over. Just understand that you will have to be stronger with your diction and language.

Diction & Language

Diction is defined as the accent, inflection, intonation and speech-sound quality manifested by an individual speaker. Simply put, when speaking "be clear". Using very clear and concise diction projects authority and builds creditability, as it speaks to an individual's level of education. The truth is, fortunately or unfortunately (depending upon how you look at it), our society has been programmed to respond more favorably to individuals with higher levels of education; so despite your education level you must expand your vocabulary and practice delivering words more concisely. Always remember, the beauty of having a job on a telephone is that people cannot make assumptions about you or your level of education until they hear you speak.

Expanding your Vocabulary

Control of a broad vocabulary can be quite powerful when leaving voicemail messages, while most collectors take this idea very lightly, and to some it's even quite humorous. I remember working as a collector, listening to my colleagues laugh at the so-called "big words" I would use when leaving a voicemail. For example, I wouldn't say *"considering the **bad** history on this file"* but, *"considering the **egregious** history on this file"*; or instead of saying, *"this isn't a **good** way to start a relationship"*, I would say, *"This isn't a very **auspicious** way to start a relationship"*. Though in both examples the former and the latter have the same meaning, I knew using the latter from both examples would command the response that I wanted (a call back). This is true because I understood the adage **"words are magic"**, was not just a cliché; empires are built on this simple idea; and if an individual (no matter their profession) understands how to use and position words effectively will find themselves at the top of the chosen profession with very little effort. Although for a collector, there are some words that cannot be used when engaging directly or leaving a voice message per (FDCPA), having a robust vocabulary will increase your effectiveness within provisions, and transform you from an average message leaver or collector to a great one.

There are many ways to expand your vocabulary, but the quickest and most effective way to develop an improved vocabulary is to start with the words you currently use. This may sound a bit strange if I'm suggesting for you to add or use different words. However, if you start with your existing language you will build a more solid foundation. The way that you will accomplish this is with the use of a thesaurus. The thesaurus is (in my experience) one of the most powerful tools known to man for vocabulary building. The reason I feel so strongly about the thesaurus is simple, it allows individuals to select terms from their current vocabulary and it provides six or seven synonyms (words that have the same meaning) to replace the word with. For instance, the word I used in the previous sentence **"replace"** the thesaurus gives eight synonyms, *put back, restore, return, reinstate, substitute, swap, trade, and change*. Having the thesaurus, as a tool of reference (if used properly) will build a strong vocabulary and make you a powerful force as a collector.

Creativity

Not only should you expand your vocabulary, it will be a must that you use your imagination. Although (FDCPA) provisions restrict deception, it does not restrict **creativity**. (FDCPA) provisions for example, restricts the uses of false titles when collecting a debt; however, I would be creative by using a title that truthfully described my job with language I knew would catch the attention of a debtor, when left on a voicemail. For instance, prior to becoming a member of management team with a first party agency collecting on delinquent car loans, as a title I would use Management Support. Using this title described my exact duties on a day-to-day basis (I supported management), so I was well within provisions. Yet, to the debtor listening to this title on a voicemail, it projected a sense of authority; in turn giving the impression that the situation may have escalated thus prompting an immediate call back.

Multiple Messages, Tone, & Consistency

Most collectors in my experience have two voicemail messages they are in control of, meaning voicemail messages where the collector knows the exact language. The first is a basic message, a simple message to have the debtor return a call; and their second message, normally an urgency message, this message usually hints at some type of possible consequence for the debtor not returning the collector's call. The problem with having control of so few voicemail messages, is after the urgency message is delivered, the debtor's situation can't get more pressing than urgent, leaving the collector with nowhere to go. As a result, there are three distinct consequences; first this forces the collector to use an ineffective freestyle way of leaving voicemail messages, where if the debtor does not return the call, and another message has to be delivered, the collector has no idea of the language or tone used on the previous voicemail left. For example, the collector could have delivered a strong tone, then soft tone, or strong language followed by soft language etc. Second, the collector after leaving his/her urgency message, has to revert back to his/her first message, only to return to the urgency message, in turn forces the collector to extreme repeat calling. Or third, the ultimate consequence, the collector is in a position after numerous unsuccessful attempts at having a debtor return a call, leaves a voicemail message that violates (FDCPA) provisions.

These are all classic cases of inconsistency, and three of the most common ways collectors lose opportunities. This is true because going around in this nonproductive circle kills creditability, thus puts the debtor in a position to call a collector's bluff. The debtor is in complete control and will pay when he/she wants to pay, (if at all). To aid you in avoiding the before explained redundancies, I will share with you a systematic process of documentation and language-tone concepts that will ensure you remain in control and consistent with the debtor when leaving voicemail messages. If you use the following process correctly, it will tremendously increase the **velocity** at which the debtor responds to your messages, meaning, instead of leaving four or five messages to have a debtor respond, you will only have to leave two maybe three. However, to appreciate and comprehend these concepts fully, you first must understand the nature of voicemail message leaving for a debt collector.

Message leaving for a debt collector at its most basic level is managing behavior; which social science teaches us that consistency is the most valuable tool when managing human behavior. **Consistency** is defined as, "an orderly presentation", so to increase the possibility of producing your desired outcome "be orderly". Understanding this idea is the first step to the three-step process.

The second step to this method would be creating at least four messages where you memorize the exact language used in each, as this will give you complete control of your messages. When developing this series of messages, keep one extremely important thing in mind; **the language on each voicemail message should escalate slightly**. Creating the messages in this fashion will accomplish two important things. First, it will ensure you do not deliver your most urgent message to soon. Secondly, it puts you in a position to use **tone** rather than just language to create **urgency** and **consistency**.

The third and final step to this process is to assign numerical ranking to each of the four-voicemail messages. Ranking your messages numerically will keep you consistent, so if the debtor does not call back after you leave a message, you know exactly what was said on the previous message and what to say and tone to use on the next. To illustrate how I used this process as a collector I had six messages in my arsenal where I knew the exact language. Each of the six messages was assigned a ranking from 1 to 6, (#1 was the least severe, #6 the most severe). After leaving my first message with the debtor, it would be documented as 1 or 1.5 (the 1.5 indicated a rank #1 message, .5 shows a stronger tone). The second message would be documented 2 or 2.5. I would continue this process using a different message, stronger tones, and more intense delivery up to the final message or until the debtor returned my call. Using this method, gave me the best possible chance of the debtor returning my call in a timely matter because it kept me consistent, credible, and in control at all times.

Also when using this process, keep in mind that you don't have to start at message #1. If you create more than the suggested four messages and document correctly you can start at message #2 or #3. There are two key points to remember if you decide to start with a stronger message. First, not to regress, meaning do not start with a rank #4 message then revert back to a rank #2 message. Second, do not deliver your most severe message(s) to soon. Moreover, only use times and/or dates, for a debtor to respond by as a last result. If you decide to leave a time and/or date on a voice message, be sure to document the event with that specific time and/or date, for that particular message. This will ensure that if the debtor does not respond, your follow up message will state the fact the debtor neglected to return your call by that time and/or date. When done properly you remain in control and consistent, thus you avoid losing creditability. Using this process in addition to principles covered in this first element will guarantee your success in the largest and most important part of your workday as a collector.

Element #2:
<u>The Talk-Off</u>

Communicate, Negotiate, Capitalize

Once a debtor calls in after listening to your effective voicemail message, this is when the real fun begins. Your voice message created an opportunity to engage with the debtor, thus affording you the chance to **Communicate**, **Negotiate**, and **Capitalize** (CNC), which is the very essence of a **Talk-off**. A **Talk-off** is a commonly used phrase in the collections industry that describes what is said to a debtor to persuade him or her to satisfy their debt. Although a Talk-off embodies communicating, negotiating and capitalizing; a Talk-off is more communicating than negotiating; and this distinction is where many collectors go wrong. Most collectors believe the primary goal for the Talk-off is to negotiate a debt; when in fact, the Talk-off is a three-part process where "negotiations" is the secondary goal. A Talk-off is "primarily" more of a tool to convince the debtor to agree to negotiate and through effective negotiating the collector would move to the final or ultimate stage of capitalizing. To bring this point in to full view, a salesman for example, would never enter the home of a prospect and immediately start discussing cost or negotiating monthly payment installments for a product or service without **first** delivering his "pitch", where the salesman will skillfully communicate and explain why the prospect can not live without the proposed product or service. When collecting a debt the same principles apply. When delivering a Talk-off, you should use persuasive language that sways the debtor to say "yes" and once that decision has been made the discussion of money can begin. Unfortunately the harsh reality is, if a collector cannot "first" convince debtors to agree to negotiate, the collector will not have an opportunity to set an arrangement; and if a collector consistently loses opportunities to capitalize, the collector will not be able to keep their job. For individuals that have not been in the business there is a certain anxiety that beginners will feel once he or she has a debtor on the phone and will usually find themselves at a lost for words "caught like a deer in headlights". This anxiety is built around the beginner not being comfortable with the prospect of asking people for their money and consequently the reason why most talent in the work force never pursues a career in the collection industry. However, if you are a beginner, follow this basic structure, and you will be able to deliver an effective Talk-off with confidence no matter how new you are to the business.

The Basic Structure of an Effective Talk-Off

- **Take control of the conversation**
- **Establish full control**
- **Disclose the reason for the call**
- **Cue the debtor to speak**
- **Have the debtor make a decision "Yes or No"**
- **Close "go for the money"**

The following is a hypothetical scenario where a secured credit card debt is being collected. It will illustrate and explain each part in this basic Talk-off structure, as well as, show you how using effective language and position can change the dynamic of a collection call.

Taking Control of a Conversation

When I interviewed potential new hires or trained an employee that was having trouble with delivering an effective Talk-off, I would have the individual(s) give me their definition of **taking control of a conversation**. The typical response was, "telling the person what to do". This is the view that is shared by most people in or outside of the industry, however this answer is incorrect. If you are considering a job as a collector or currently a collector, you must have a clear understanding of this concept, because this concept is at the core of your success at delivering an effective Talk-off. **Taking or having control of the conversation simply means, when you are speaking, the debtor is listening; and when the debtor speaks, it is because you gave the debtor permission with a cue, by way of a question.** This is the most important concept in a Talk-off structure, because there is no way you can effectively deliver a Talk-off if you are going back and forth, playing verbal ping-pong with the debtor. Understand, for every word the debtor speaks during your Talk-off that is not prompted by a cue, the percentage of you having the debtor satisfy the debt is decreased. Once you have a firm grasp of this concept, you will know at what point you are losing control and can **reposition** and regain control. For instance, if the debtor starts to speak before your cue, you say *"Maim/ Sir, we both can't talk at the same time, I am required to explain this information, so that you are clear on your options. You will have an opportunity to give your side once I'm done and you will have my full attention",* Now you are back in the driver's seat. Never go back and forth with the debtor, because it increases the likelihood of the call escalating, thus turning the conversation into a shouting match further increasing the odds of you NOT receiving a payment to satisfy the debt.

The First Step to Taking Control "Reposition"

When the debtor returns your call, it is important to understand your position. The debtor took time out of their busy day to find out the reason for your call and will usually open with "*what is this all about?*". At this point the debtor is in control, meaning the debtor posed the first question. When this question is asked, you have to **reposition**, which means **getting in a position where you are asking the questions**; this will be easy since the debtor is willing to listen, after responding to your effective message. The way to **reposition** and establish control is by first placing the debtor on hold, and then return to the call. A large number of collectors make the mistake of not placing the debtor on hold while pulling the debtor's account information for fear that the debtor will hang up before they have a chance to deliver their Talk-off. Never attempt this, doing so only gives the debtor an opportunity to ask more questions, which is the last thing that you want before you reposition. The debtor will never hang up until he or she has a clear idea of what the call is about (if the voicemail was left properly). Take advantage of this time by placing the debtor on hold, pull the account and survey the debtor's information, gather your thoughts and compose yourself for Talk-off delivery. Don't rush **reposition** and stay calm.

Establishing Full Control

Once you return to the phone, this is when you **establish full control**. First disclose who you are (your name) and your agency's name and no other information. Never lead with the company that your agency is representing before establishing full control, because once the debtor hears the creditor's name, he/she will have an idea what the call is about and could possibly make a decision to disconnect the call. The goal at this point would be to have the debtor get something to write with. **To ensure that you have complete control, it is essential that the debtor is writing while you are speaking**. Remember, you haven't given any information beyond your name and the name of your agency, so the debtor is still clueless as to what your call is about, and will follow your lead to get more information. You say, "*Do you have something to write with? I'm required to give you your assigned file number before I disclose any information*". The debtor will concede to this because not writing down this number is keeping them from hearing the reason for your strong message and in most cases, they really want you to get on with it. Once the debtor has something to write with you have won the first battle of establishing full control.

Note: *When you provide the account number for the debtor to write down, **you should always** end the account number with the last four digits of the debtor social security number, and ask "that should be the last four of your social . . . correct?". Doing this will confirm that you are talking the* *right person as well as ensure that the debtor cannot deny the neglected obligation once you start delivering your Talk-off.*

Disclose the reason for the call, but "DON'T GO FOR THE MONEY"

One of the biggest mistakes made when attempting to collect a debt is a collector going for the money to soon. This may sound a little ridiculous at first thought, because this is what you are paid to do. However, instead of the collector asking for, or discussing money, the collector will first ask for a statement from the debtor, as to the neglect of the debt. What this does is change the dynamic of the collections call. This tactic will set the debtor in the thought process of **"what can I do to stop what ever is happening?"**. I found this to be true because debt collectors in recent years have been so aggressive that debtors are somewhat taken by surprise if a collector does not out right ask for the money immediately and **even though you will not say it**, the debtor will suspect something else may be happening. I have used this approach for years and have had debtors almost beg me to take their money before I got to the end of this Talk-off.

Note: *For third party collectors, before disclosing the reason for the call you are required (**per FDCPA provisions**) to deliver the Mini Miranda.*

To accomplish this, you must maintain control and state the creditor your agency is representing followed by what transpired between these two parties. Only say your agency name once, as this will keep the conversation directed to the issue between (**the creditor**) and (**the debtor**), thus keeping you from having to defend the role of your company; which if you let happen, will switch the conversation away from the debt in question. **Remember, your company is just the liaison.** You will continue with the debtor's actions, and how the creditor views the debtor's actions or the lack thereof, and explain that you have to document the file with a statement. For instance, *"We are calling on the behalf of (**credit card company's name**), you were provided a line of credit, while allowing you to use your bank account as collateral. However, when (**the credit card company's name**) attempted to retrieve the funds the bank account was closed . . . Now, because you close the account and made no attempt to repay, (**the credit card company's name**) will be taking the position that you had no intention of paying this debt at all. There are a couple of questions I have to ask you to document the file appropriately before (**the credit card company's name**) moves forward . . . the first of which is . . ."* Notice how the language used and delivery maintained control, explained the situation, and kept the issue between the two parties. It also leads the debtor to the opportunity to speak.

Cue the debtor to speak

This is the point where you give permission for the debtor to speak, however controlled. The way to maintain control when prompting a debtor to speak is by **asking questions that you know the answer to**. I'm not suggesting you know verbatim what the debtor will say, just a general idea of the type of answer to expect and to make sure the debtor doesn't answer outside of the questions. Just as a lawyer that is cross examining, the attorney stays in complete control by never asking questions that he/she does not know the answer to; and they never allow the person being cross examined to speak unless he/she gives a cue with a question. There should be two questions, the first should be, **why the debtor mislead the creditor,** and second, **why the debtor has not handled the debt voluntarily before now.** It is extremely important to be documenting or at least giving the impression that you are documenting as the debtor is speaking. You continue, "*Mr. Doe is there any particular reason why the bank account was closed?* "**Document response. Second question . . .**" *Mr. Doe is there any reason why you haven't taken care of this before now?*" **Document response**. This puts you in a position of power because it sends the message to the debtor that this matter may be a foregone conclusion, "**the creditor may be taking action**". In most cases, if done properly, the debtor will be thinking, "**what can I do to stop what ever is happening**", and will say, "*Well, how much is it?*" Again I say, DON'T GO FOR THE MONEY . . . stick to your guns, and continue documenting. You say, "*Maim/Sir, I am required to document the file appropriately, we will get to a point where you can take care of this matter voluntarily*" . . . This is important because continuing to document even after money was suggested sends the impression that the money isn't your goal or the issue.

Have the debtor make a simple "yes or no" decision

After your documentation is complete, the goal is to have the debtor make a simple yes or no decision, (nothing in between). Debtors that are reluctant to handle their obligations are very good at giving creative sob stories and will invite you to a piece of pie at their pity party; where the debtor will explain why they have not paid, "*I would have **but**", and will talk you right off the phone. Although showing a little empathy can help in moving you to your ultimate goal, having the debtor give you a simple yes or no will keep you in control and put you in position to effectively negotiate an arrangement. So before you have a taste of that pity pie, you would say, "*Mr. Doe, we are required to give you one last opportunity to take care of this voluntarily, as a result your file can be placed into a **compliance** or **noncompliance** status, and I am required to explain both. **Compliance** is where we workout a payment arrangement and you handle this voluntarily or **noncompliance**, where you say, I understand my rights and I will much rather face (**give the possible consequences**)*". Notice how the Talk-off structure in combination with position and persuasive language leads the debtor to a yes or no answer (compliance or noncompliance) without discussing money. This is important because you always lead with the debtor's neglect of the issue. However, the battle is not over, this was not the close. Once the debtor states that he or she wants to comply, you simply state, *"Mr. Doe, I have to let management know that you decided to handle this on a voluntary basis . . . please hold"*. **Place the debtor on hold**.

Placing the debtor on hold a second time will accomplish three things. First, you will see if the debtor is serious about handling the debt, or if the debtor is just waiting for the opportunity to hang up the phone. Second, it will give the impression that you are discussing the matter with a higher authority. Lastly, it gives you a break between discussing the issue and discussing money, thus putting yourself in a much better position for the second stage of the Talk-off **"negotiations"** and closing on an arrangement. Because you have listened and documented the reasons why the debtor has not taken care of the debt, you should have an idea of their ability to pay.

The Close . . . "Going for the money"

Notice through out this process the amount of the debt has not been discussed, nor when it will have to be paid. The only thing has been accomplished is by using persuasive language and position (taking and maintaining control of the conversation) the debtor has been somewhat influenced to say "yes". As I mentioned before, you have been listening and to some extent determined the debtor's ability to pay, i.e. if the debtor is working or if he/she have some type of income. Remember, the violin will come out, so stay focused, tell them how much, and set an arrangement.

Build rapport but stay firm

Rapport building is extremely important when collecting debt, yet it is necessary that you stay firm throughout the Talk-off. An attempt to build rapport should be pursued only after a decision to satisfy the debt has been made and in turn accomplish three things. First, it should take a little pressure off of the situation to avoid escalating the call when negotiating a payment arrangement. Second, it is a way to build trust before asking for the debtor's banking information; and finally, it should help you position your payment arrangement as a priority over all others without being hostile. Remember, you are not the only person competing for the debtor's money, so making your arrangement first in line will be your objective. However, while building rapport, I'm not suggesting that you be "buddy buddy" with the debtor, because making a friend is the fastest way to have your arrangement broken or made less important. Yet, don't be so firm that if the debtor, after making an arrangement with you for some reason doesn't have the money, or maybe has just a portion, he or she will not pick up the phone and talk to you about it. Performing this balancing act between firm professionalism and good rapport will keep the debtor communicating with you, which is key because you cannot collect money from a debtor you cannot talk to.

Getting the bank information

When attempting to persuade a debtor to provide their banking information over the telephone it is important to understand that, on the most basic level, one person is calling another person out of the clear blue and within minutes will be asking for an individual's most personal asset beyond their first born. From this fundamental view, the debtor should have cause for suspicion. Not to mention, TV show after TV show explaining to consumers why they should never under any circumstance provide their personal banking information over the phone to someone he or she does not know. This is mainly due to the many cases of fraud that have been reported in recent years, and debtor will use this as a crutch to avoid setting up an arrangement. That being said, overcoming this hurtle can be difficult; nevertheless, the goal is to have the debtor pay the debt in the most efficient way possible, which means refusal to set up an arrangement "NOW", is not an option. Remember, a compliance or noncompliance ultimatum was given and the debtor chose to comply, so if a fight erupts, you will use their decision to comply to your advantage. Furthermore, you have to make the reason behind the debtor providing the information makes sense. **Redirecting** will help you achieve this.

Redirecting

First you want to ask for the information directly, *Maim/Sir will you be setting this up by check, visa or master card?* Again, because of the creditability you have built and the control that you established, there is a 50/50 chance that the debtor will just set it up without a fight. However, if the debtor puts up a fight, the way you handle it in a non-combative way would be to **redirect**.

Redirecting is a process where a collector will overcome an objection by quickly bringing the debtor back to the possible consequences of not paying the debt voluntarily, and again have the debtor commit to a simple yes/no decision. For example, *"Mr./Ms Doe, I understand exactly how you feel, however . . . because the length of time it took to make contact with you, in addition to your neglect of this issue, you can't simply tell me a date in the future when you feel funds will be available. When I make contact, explain the situation and document the file appropriately, I am required to either place your file in a **compliance** or **noncompliance** status . . . so depending upon if we can come to an agreement will determine how the **(creditor's name)** will pursue the matter . . . . And I was under the impression that you wanted to comply"*. This example of redirecting not only brings the debtor back to a yes or no decision, it also reminds the debtor of the neglect, as well as hints at the debtor facing the possible consequences. After **redirecting** in this fashion, in most cases, the debtor will concede.

If the debtor doesn't have a bank account

Another way collectors miss opportunities to capitalize in an attempt to collect a debt would be not knowing how to close on a payment arrangement if the debtor does not have a bank account. To illustrate, a collector for example, will go through his/her Talk-off and convinces the debtor to agree to pay, only to find out that the debtor doesn't have a bank account. The collector, after hearing this news, generally feels as though they lost the deal; because they know through past experiences a debtor sending a money order via mail in a reasonable time frame is highly unlikely, if they send it at all, *"What's your address? I'll send it through the mail"* (YEA RIGHT!). If the debtor doesn't have a bank account this is no excuse for not (at least) setting up an arrangement today or within 24 hours. To increase the chances of you getting a payment if the debtor does not have a bank account would be to have the debtor purchase a prepaid green dot card. These cards are extremely easy to obtain and can be purchased at any department store such as CVS, Wal-Mart or Walgreen's. The cards are inexpensive, and can be purchased for about five dollars. Most importantly, the card can be purchased without the funds for the arrangement being available.

Persuading the debtor to purchase a prepaid Green-dot card increases the chances of you receiving the payment for three important reasons. First, it starts the process of the debtor making the payment. Second, the debtor having possession of the card is a constant reminder of arrangement that he or she agreed to. Lastly, you are giving the debtor an easy and low cost way that helps them avoid the possible consequences until he or she will have the funds available. What you will say is *"Maim/Sir, what we do to help individuals who don't have a bank accounts is allow them to use prepaid Green-dot Cards . . . are you familiar with the cards? . . .* **wait for the answer** *"yes" . . . they cost between 3 and 5 dollars and you don't have to have the funds on the card to purchase it . . . what we need is the 16 digit code on the card to set the arrangement and get you into compliance . . . I can allow a 24-hour period after making contact and explaining the situation before I have to place your account in one of the two statuses.* **Further explain that,** *"the reason we give only a 24 hour window Mr/Ms. Doe, is because the cards are so inexpensive and so easy to find, if a person is not willing to do something so simple as to purchase the card when we don't require the funds to be available,* **(the creditor's name)** *feel as though the person is not serious about taking care of the debt, so they don't waste time and move forward . . .*

Why give 24-hours to purchase a prepaid if the debtor does not have the money today?

The reason for the, **24 hour time frame**, is to capitalize on the urgency that has been built. You literally have one shot to start the debtor in the process of making the payment. You are not the only problem in their lives and certainly not the only person asking for their money. The last thing that you want is for the debtor to get off the phone and allow the issue to become less important, because the debtor most certainly will turn into a no contact. So having the debtor agree to "at least" start the process of making the payment even though they may not have the money today will be key.

Avoid setting the debtor up for failure

Once the debtor agrees to set the arrangement and gives their banking or credit card information, remember you don't have the money yet, just a promise to pay, the same thing the creditor had that your agency is representing; and the reason you have a job. **Getting a promise to pay is not what makes you a good collector. Getting the debtor to keep the promise makes you a good collector.**

The best way to increase the likelihood of a debtor keeping his/her promise to pay would be to not set the debtor up for failure. The previous Talk-off structure though subtle is high pressure and you can, (without knowing or trying) set the debtor with a promise he/she cannot keep. Like I mentioned before, you should have listened and have somewhat determined the debtor's ability to pay; so if the debtor tells you he/she can pay $2,000.00 on Friday and he or she works part time at Wendy's, the chances of you getting the $2,000.00 is highly unlikely. The way to avoid this situation is to make the debtor be honest with you. You say, *"Mr./Ms. Doe, please understand because of the situation that we are in, there is a zero tolerance for returned item. In the case of a returned item, this arrangement will be forfeited and (the creditor's name) will possibly move forward with legal action . . . so the last thing we want to do is set an individual up to fail. So be honest, if you will not be able to pay this amount say it now, so we can find an arrangement within reason".* After using this approach the debtor in most cases will be honest and will make a decision on what he/she can pay, not on pressure that you have created.

Element #3:
<u>Rebuttals</u>

Note: *As we discussed in the Talk-off chapter, if you have properly taken control you significantly reduce the chances of having to overcome an objection beyond I don't have the money. However, there are certain debtors you will engage with that will put up a fight no matter how well you have maintained control.*

Rebuttals are defined as an attempt to disarm an opponent argument. In the world of collections a collector will use rebuttals to overcome objections. Debtors use objections as ammunition to avoid paying a debt, and depending on how well you "as a collector" react to objections will play a huge role in determining how successful you will be at collecting. Understanding how to overcome a debtor's objections using effective rebuttals will be absolutely essential to performing at a high level collecting debt. This is an area where many opportunities are lost, because most collectors are not familiar with the most basic rebutting techniques, and as a result, lose control allowing the call to escalate.

Never let the debtor escalate the call

Note: *The easiest way to avoid an escalated call is to stay within (FDCPA) provisions. In most cases, debtors know the most common laws when it come to collecting a debt and if the debtor feels as though you violated a provision, you will find yourself defending your actions and not discussing the debt. Violating FDCPA provisions is a breeding ground for an escalated call, so avoiding this is the first step to reducing the chances of producing an escalated situation.*

A debtor's escalation of a call is not a textbook objection, it's more of a tactic used by a debtor to start an argument to justify hanging up the phone without making a rational decision. As a collector the last thing you want to happen is for the debtor to disconnect the call, because the phone conversation is the only thing that keeps you in position to have the debtor to satisfy the debt. There was a time when mobsters would kill the people that owed a debt; until they realized that a dead man doesn't have the ability to pay, so they started breaking arms and legs. This is a somewhat demonstrative way of looking at it, however, if you allow the debtor to bait you into an argument and they disconnect the call to you the debtor is dead; this is true because you lost your means to communicate, negotiate, and capitalize on an arrangement. Never play in to this, if a debtor attempts to use this tactic, a light should pop on in your head making you aware that this person's goal is to avoid paying their debt. This debtor understands that if an argument ensues they have a reason not to talk to you, and if they don't talk to you, they don't have to figure out a way to satisfy their neglected obligation.

Feel, Felt, Found

The way to avoid the call escalation trap beyond staying within (FDCPA) provisions is to first remain calm. No matter how loud or unruly the debtor becomes, don't match it, and stay on script. By staying calm you keep creditability and disarm the debtor. A great tactic to use to stay on script is the **Feel, Felt, Found,** technique. This tactic was developed in the sales industry as a way to overcome objections of a prospect showing signs of not purchasing a product or service a salesman was trying to sell. Using this technique when attempting to collect a debt, you will be redirecting the debtor to the possible consequences of not paying the debt. For example, say the debtor didn't want to give their bank information over the phone and you insist that the debtor provides it. This is a very sensitive area because a person's banking information is extremely personal and can cause a debtor to become emotional. You would say, *"Mr/Ms Doe, I know exactly how you **FEEL**, as a matter of fact I **FELT** the same way, however what I **FOUND** working in this business is that, individuals that make the mistake of not setting up an arrangement, in most cases regret it because (**followed by the possible consequences**).* Using this technique will keep you calm, on script, and increases the likelihood of you overcoming the objection.

Note: *The Talk-off structure is designed to have the debtor assume the debt. So if you properly maintain control the chances of having to overcome these objections are tremendously reduced.*

This debt does not belong to me

In the case that you are collecting on a debt that is two years old or older, the debtor will on occasion, try to deny the debt by stating **the debt does not belong to them** or **they paid the debt off**. In the collection industry this can happen, however this is true in very few cases. Nine times out of ten the debt will be valid. The most commonly used rebuttal for this situation would be to give a "**clear & complete**". A **clear and complete** is a method used by collectors to identify the debtor, through verifying the debtor's personal information from the account such as, birth date, social security number, and/or previous bank information. This method can be effective, though be careful when providing certain information from the debtor's file, because doing so is one of the quickest ways to lose a deal. As mentioned earlier, the information will be older and may have traveled to several agencies; consequently on occasion, leaving some information incomplete e.g. transposed numbers, incorrect previous bank name, or incorrect previous place of employment. For instance, in the case of previous bank name, when the agency runs the routing number on file for the debtor, it gives Wells Fargo, now when you provide this information to the debtor he/she will say "*I never had an account with Well Fargo*" and they haven't, because what we didn't know is Wachovia was bought out by Well Fargo and now you have lost creditability and the debtor may not give you a chance to recover and hang up.

The most effective way to handle this situation is not to jump in and start providing information . . . but only suggest that the information is available. You will also want to **redirect** the debtor to making a simple yes/no decision of weather or not he/she want to run the risk of facing the possible consequences if the debtor is trying to deceive you. For example, the debtor will say, "*this is not my debt*" you will reply by saying "*Mr./Ms. Doe, we work directly with* (*the creditor's name*) *corporate office and we have a legal team that verifies all of the information and send out letters to the address listed before we call . . . my job is to make contact, explain the situation, document the file appropriately and have you make a decision on if you want to handle this matter on a voluntary basis, or if you want* (*the possible consequences*). *However, I will say that considering the information* (*the creditor's name*) *has . . . your social security number, your exact date of birth, and your previous banking information, this is pretty much an open and close. Now, Mr./Ms Doe do you want to go in to a compliance or noncompliance, because if this becomes a legal matter you will have the burden of proofing this debt does not belong to you*" . . . Notice the way this rebuttal brings the debtor back to yes or no, and only suggest that the information is available, instead of giving any information from the file.

I paid this debt off

When the debtor states that a debt was paid off, as I aforementioned, the chances of their claim being true, though not impossible, is highly unlikely. The best defense against this type of objection will be to not only have the debtor show documented proof of the debt being satisfied, but also give a short time frame to show proof. In my experience, debtors that have satisfied a debt do not waste time proving it, and will not give you the run-a-round to clear their name. However, the debtor that makes this claim and is not telling the truth, (please understand) this is not their first rodeo and has more than likely played this game before. This type of debtor will use this tactic in an attempt to prolong the situation and you will most certainly lose contact. You would say, "*Mr./Ms Doe unfortunately due to your neglect of this issue, and the length of time it took to make contact, once we explain your options, and document your file, we only have a 24-48 hour time frame to come to an agreement and have an arrangement set . . . So if you have proof of this debt has been satisfied, It has to be faxed to me within that time period, or I will have to place your file into a **noncompliance** status*". Again, this redirects the debtor back to (the possible consequences), and if the debtor is not telling the truth, you remind him/her that you documented and gave them a chance to handle the situation on a voluntary basis.

The take away close

Often times when negotiating a debt, the debtor will give a ridiculous amount for the payment arrangement, such as $10.00 a month to satisfy a $6,000.00 obligation and will stand firm, stating they can not afford more. Basically this type of objection is a tactic used by debtors to prompt an escalated call. This is true because the debtor knows the proposed amount is unreasonable and more times than less will not be accepted. With this type of objection the debtor is searching for a reason not to talk to you. Again, this is another classic case of a debtor trying to avoid paying a debt and to overcome this type of objection, you would use ***the take away close***. This is another technique used in the sales industry where the salesman while negotiating, gives the illusion to the prospect that the deal will be taken off the table, and reminding the prospect of the benefits that he/she will be losing by not accepting a proposed offer. This tactic can be extremely powerful if used correctly when collecting a debt. The most important thing to remember when using this technique is to remain calm, and act as though you can care less if the debtor agrees to a reasonable arrangement or not. Using this method you will redirect the debtor back to the possible consequences, while reminding them of the opportunity and money that will be wasted not taking advantage of your courtesy call. For instance, *Mr. Doe unfortunately I will not be able to accept those arrangements, this is just a courtesy call, somewhat of a last opportunity you have to handle this before it becomes a possible legal matter. However, I will say that you will lose more money due to legal fees and court cost, **if** the situation becomes a legal matter. But this is your decision, and we don't force people to take advantage"*. Politely say, *"We will be sending correspondence to your home address, thank you"* and disconnect the call. Moreover, the use of this technique gives way to another tactic developed in the sales world, most used by strong negotiators called **reducing to the ridiculous**. This approach when collecting a debt uses the facts of the possible consequences to overcoming an objection by explaining to the debtor why not handling the debt on a voluntary basis is almost absurd. If done correctly the debtor will definitely call back to discuss more reasonable arrangements.

Element #4:
<u>The Reference Relay</u>

The concept of the Reference Relay

The Reference Relay is a phrase that I coined to explain the concept of using persuasive language and position to create enough urgency to convince a third party to help a collector locate and make contact with the debtor. As you will learn in the world of collections this is not an easy job. The fact is, third parties hate debt collectors, the reason third parties hate collectors is they themselves are debtors, and certainly do not want to be bothered with someone else's collections calls. The reality is debtors are on teams, and a third party will not help you if they suspect that you are collecting a debt. However, there are concepts and/or principles that I created that you can follow that will make you more proficient at getting your message to the debtor with the help of a third party.

(FDCPA) provisions are very clear as to what a collector can or cannot say to a third party. For this reason, most collectors are often reluctant to call or even engage with a third party, for fear of violating (FDCPA) provisions. Collectors are also hesitant to call or engage with a third party because of past failures, where a third party may have hung the phone up on the collector or maybe had to endure abusive language. As a consequence of this reluctance, collectors are not taking full advantage of every potential avenue to make contact with the debtor, thus losing a tremendous amount of opportunities to capitalize. Understanding the enormous prospective dollars that can be generated if a collector can consistently convince a third party to relay a message that will influence the debtor to call in is essential; because if you can become proficient at this, your debtor contact can potentially double. The reason your debtor contact will potentially double is very simple, the design of the loan application. The design of the typical loan application calls for two or three third party phone numbers for every one-debtor phone number. Using simple math this means, you are twice or three times as likely to have first contact with a third party than a debtor. Considering this information, if you want your production to double, you must master the art of the Reference Relay. To help you master this art I put together simple principles to follow to increase the likelihood of your desire result.

Create solid third party messages

We discussed in the voicemail message leaving chapter the importance of the voicemail messages for the debtor. The same principles will apply when leaving a message for the reference. You will have to create at least two messages that are designed specifically for a third party. This is very important because most collectors have one basic message for the third party, which is the "**you were put down as a reference**" message. When creating the two messages, they should not be hostile. The reason these messages should never be hostile is if the third party returns your call after listening to a hostile message, you will find yourself in a position using the opportunity to defend your message, instead of getting the third party to help you. When creating these messages you should accomplish three goals. First the messages should tie the parties together. Second, the messages should not disclose any information or any hint that a debt is being collected. Third, they should create a subtle sense of urgency to prompt an immediate call back.

The initial third party message

As we discussed earlier the information on the debtor's file will be about 2 years old or older and may have some errors. Considering this, the phone number present for the third party may be the phone number for the debtor. This will be used to your advantage because your initial message will include both names on the voicemail. Having both party's names on the first message is extremely important because it ties the two parties together and takes advantage of the history between the two, whether the history is good or bad. Secondly, the initial message should be vague in nature. This vagueness will ensure that you do not disclose any information or give any hint that the message is an attempt to collect a debt. Again I stress, a third party will not help you if they sense you are collecting a debt. Furthermore, the message design for the third party isn't an attempt to collect a debt; it is designed to simply have the third party return the call. So your goal will be to use persuasive language to have the third party return your call, nothing more. Lastly, the message should create a slight sense of urgency. This sense of urgency will be created with the language, tone and delivery of the message. Keep in mind; you want an immediate call back so choosing word and word phrase combinations that commands a prompt response will be essential.

.

As an example of how to leave an initial message that incorporates all three concepts I designed the following message. *"This message is for **John Doe** or **Mary Land**, my name is(**Your name**), I'm calling in reference to a matter that has arisen in our office that requires **your immediate attention**. I will be the **last person that will see this file before it leaves our office**, so it will be important that you get in contact with me as soon as you receive this message (followed by your contact information).* This message is well within the (FDCPA) provisions, and accomplishes three goals, first it ties the two parties together, secondly, it's vague and does not disclose any information other than your name and contact number, and lastly, it gives a sense of urgency to call back.

Don't sound like a collector

When engaging with a third party the last thing you want is to sound like you are collecting a debt. This may sound a little bizarre because your ultimate goal will be to collect a debt; however the third party does not know this. In fact, the FDCPA third party provision plays to your advantage, because it restricts third party disclosure. Plus as I mention earlier, third parties hate collectors, and will not help you if they suspect you are attempting to collect a debt. So if sounding like a collector reduces the chances of the third party helping you and increases the likelihood of you getting cursed out . . . why sound like one? This is an extremely important principle to understand because collectors are notorious for dead giveaways when engaging with a third party. Though there are many ways in which collectors give clues that would lead a third party to believe a debt is being collected, the most notable give-a-way would be the collector using the phrase *"you were put down as a reference"*. Because this phrase has been used so much over the years when leaving a message or engaging with a third party, when the third party hears it, they know exactly what the call is about. The funny thing is, nowhere in the (FDCPA) provision does it require a collector when engaging with a third party, to use this phrase. If you want to be successful at the Reference Relay the first thing you must do is remove this phrase from your repertoire.

Be Pleasant

One of the most common misconceptions among collectors when engaging with a third party is being rude would be the best way to have a third party deliver a message to the debtor to prompt the debtor to call in. This method can be effective in some cases, (**though I do not recommend it**). However, the problem with using this tactic is when the third party contacts the debtor, after a unpleasant experience with a debt collector, the third party will be upset, in turn causing the debtor to be upset. As a result, starting your opportunity to capitalize with an escalated call, and like we explained in the Rebuttals Element, the likelihood of you getting an arrangement is tremendously reduce. Understand, the one (FDCPA) provision consumers know more than any other, is that a collector cannot disclose to or abuse a third party. That being said, your goal will be to accomplish one important thing, **to use language, diction and position so effectively that without you even giving the third party a clear reason as to why, he or she immediately calls the debtor once disconnecting with you, and explain to the debtor how important it is that you are contacted as soon as possible.**

The open for an Effective Reference Relay

Note: *Like we learned in the talk off chapter, taking and maintaining control will be key to achieving your desire result after getting the debtor on the phone. The same principles apply when you are talking to a third party; taking control of the conversation is your first line of business.*

Because of the way the previous hypothetical message was designed and the tone delivered, to a certain degree it may portray a sense of involvement of the third party; and after listening, the third party in most case may be thinking, *"what is going on and how am I involved?"*. This puts you in perfect position for two reasons; first the third party will be ready to listen to what you have to say; second, the third party will be relieved once you let them know they have no involvement and will be more willing to help you. When the third party calls in he/she will usually state their name only and most times will not mention the debtors name. He/she will open with *"this is Mary Land, I am returning a call for the message you left for me"*. You will say, *"was it another name associated with the voicemail?"*, the third party will say *"yes, John Doe"*. Like we discussed earlier in the Talk-off chapter you will want to take control of the conversation, by first placing the third party on hold, you reply *"Mr. Doe? Ok . . . hold briefly while I pull that file"*. Remember, to avoid running the risk of giving too much information this will be short and sweet. The conversation should be no more than five minutes. You will attempt to verify the debtor's employment and residential information; however, the only information you will be giving is an account number, your name and a direct contact number, all of which the third party will write down nothing else, not even your company name if possible. It's important that the third party writes down the information because it serves as a constant reminder to deliver your message; plus, it ensures that you are in control of the conversation. While the reference is on hold, pull the information, gather your thoughts and prepare for delivery.

When the third party returns to the phone stay focused and in control give the account number and your direct phone number. He/she may have multiple questions, however the only one that you will address is the question of their involvement, which you will quickly assure them they have no connection. Stick to script, you want them off the phone as quickly as possible. If he/she asks a question out side of their involvement, your response will be *"unfortunately I cannot disclose the details of the situation, all of our calls are recorded, however Mr. Doe needs to contact me today to give his side of the story"*. Thank them and politely disconnect the call.

Avoid disclosing to a spouse

Debtors will frequently use their spouse as a reference, which isn't bad for you because he/she in most cases has total access to the debtor. However, avoid disclosing what the call is about and never attempt to deliver your Talk-off. The reason you should never attempt this is first, the debt does not belong to the spouse, and therefore he/she will not be setting up an arrangement with you without talking to the debtor first. Secondly, **the spouse is not trained to deliver your talk-off** and will not use the principles we discussed in the Talk-off chapter. More times than less the spouse will simply tell the debtor that a bill collector called (if he/she tell the debtor at all). If you let this happen the debtor will make a decision not to pay without discussing it with you first. I have listened to countless collectors make this mistake, because of the spouse's persistency, or even threatened, that will not relay a message without more information. Don't fall for this, if you are faced with this threat, simply tell the spouse, *"That's fine sir/maim, I will document the file that you were advised to relay the message, and you refused. However please understand, all of our calls are recorded, so if this situation escalates and he/she is confronted with this matter, we have your refusal on record . . . thanks sir maim have a good day".* Because you stated the fact that you documented as well as the conservation was recorded, puts pressure on the spouse to relay your message.

Element #5:
<u>File Management</u>

"Discovery consists of seeing what everybody has seen and
thinking what nobody has thought".
Albert Von Szent Gyorgyi

File management is the most important area of all, because this is the element, where all the previously discussed components come together and you see exactly how complete or incomplete you are as a collector. In essence, this is where efficiency, productivity, and effectiveness meet, thus giving you a clear picture of **strengths** as well as any **weaknesses** within your arsenal. As you will soon find out, due to limitations of collection management teams, there will be zero time spent on finding your weak points; therefore understanding this area and implementing the system I designed to help you properly manage a file will be of extreme importance. However, before we discuss the purpose and importance of effective file management, it is essential that you know how a collection file is created, so that you have a clear understanding of the process.

Defining File Management

When a creditor (such as a bank) owns debt that has been pursued for a certain period of time (usually one to two years) and the debt has not been successfully collected, the creditor will deem the debt uncollectible and in turn the delinquent accounts are **charged-off.** Once the debt is charged-off the creditor then bundles the uncollected accounts into what's called a **portfolio** (a series of uncollected accounts packaged by a creditor) and sends it to the market to be sold or assigns it to a collection agency.

When a collections agency receives a portfolio through **consignment**, (where the original creditor assigns the debt to a third party agency to be collected) or through **purchase**, (where the agency purchases and owns the debt outright), it is broken down into sections. These sections are then assigned to the collectors, and referred to as a **collection file or list**. Working a **collections file** describes the process of dialing numbers provided on the individual accounts, in conjunction with the use of **status codes** (an acronym used to describe a specific action taken on an account) and **documenting** (notations describing the action taken in more detail) to maximize the file's full potential, meaning generate as much money as possible during a given time period, in most cases a month. This process of calling, using status codes, and documenting is referred to as **File Management**.

Unfortunately, the area of **File Management** has been grossly underserved. The industry as a whole has not realized the true potential of the properly managed file and the information that it is capable of producing. Though there are multiple reasons for this area's neglect, nevertheless it will be essential that you understand the two reasons that through my years in this industry, I found to be the root cause. The first would be the industry not fully understanding what constitutes a collector's effectiveness and second the limitations of collections software.

Effectiveness

A common misconception in this industry is that the individual that generates the most money is considered the most effective, yet this is not always the case. This suggestion may seem a bit lofty, or even a bit idealistic to most individuals in the industry. However, if you feel this way, it's because you are only asking yourself only one out of the two important questions when measuring the performance of a collector, which is **how much money is this collector generating in comparison to his/her counterparts.** The often overlooked and I would argue the most important question that you are not considering is **how many opportunities is a collector losing due to an existing weakness.** Asking this second and all important question should bring into focus the reality that the collector that generates the most money could very well be costing a company far more than he or she is producing. To illustrate this point, say that two collectors, Collector A, and Collector B were collecting on small balance credit cards; and for the month of April, Collector A collected $10,000.00 and Collector B collected $7,000.00. From this fundamental view it would appear that Collector A is the employee of the month and Collector B should be trying to find out what Collector A is doing right. However, what we didn't know is Collector A had a much more lucrative file in terms of direct contact phone numbers and missed another $10,000.00 in the first week due to poor voicemail message leaving. While Collector B on the other hand, only misses $2,500.00 the first week, because the debtors were unemployed. (We will revisit this scenario to show in detail how Collector A lost $10,000.00 in a week in the **vagueness of the status codes** section that follows). This brief illustration is to show high dollar amounts though seductive, should not be used as the only measure of effectiveness, a concept we call **numbers hiding the numbers**.

Numbers hiding the numbers

Numbers hiding the numbers is a concept that describes how high dollar amounts overshadows the ratios that truly show how effective or ineffective a collector is when working a file. Not understanding this concept is why agency management teams are often clueless as to how a collector can be the top collector one month and the next at the bottom. Management usually will chalk this situation up as the collector got lazy or didn't work as hard because of the previous month success; when in fact, the collector may have worked just as hard or harder. However, the collector's bad habits and/or not being aware that a particular weakness exists, may have caught up with them, and as a result, would not keep the collector consistent.

The limitation of collections software

Collections software is (in most cases) user friendly, as it should be since collecting a debt is not rocket science Like the goal for any software, it is designed to help the end user manage his/her workload more efficiently, thus a tool to measure and enhance productivity. Productivity enhancements are good enough for most any call center type of job; however, **due to the nature of working a collections file, where every conversation with a debtor, third party or any action taken on a specific account is potentially connected to an agency's bottom-line,** enhanced productivity is only half of what I consider necessary to satisfy an end user collector. The half that is missing is enhancements in collection software that measure effectiveness beyond a broken promise. The reality is, a highly productive ineffective collector can cost an agency thousands of dollars on a daily basis, this is true because going faster will not fix ineffectiveness issues.

Although we will be launching collections software designed to address these and many other limitations for the end user collector, as a substitute I have created an easy to understand manual system of using status codes that will help you manage a collections file more effectively. This system if used properly will give you the much needed analytical information required to reveal any weakness you may have that we discussed in the previous four core elements.

Before we dive into the system and how it works, there are a couple issues that must be addressed to make sure the process is maximized to its full potential. I explained earlier that a status code was an acronym used to describe a specific action taken on an account by a collector; however, there are two issues I have with the way in which the status codes are being used, the first of which is **the vagueness of the codes.**

Vagueness of status codes

The status codes currently being used in the industry are far too vague. Though these codes give a hint as to what happened, they do not paint a detailed enough picture, consequently forcing the collector or manager to waste time to search for more details. For instance, consider for a moment the status code LM (Left Message on voicemail), a commonly used status code. If you were to glance at this status code would you say it means the collector left a message with the debtor or third party? Does it mean the collector left a message on a good number, where the debtor or third party is identified by name on the voicemail or left a message on a possible phone number, where the debtor or third party is not identified by name on the voicemail? This type of ambiguity leads to inefficiencies, i.e. double work, disconnect between collectorand file being worked, disconnect between management and collectors, which will cost you as well as the agency time and money.

Secondly, status codes are not being used to measure effectiveness. Once you understand that status codes should be designed to give more detailed information about a specific action taken, it will be easy for you to understand how they can be used to measure effectiveness. To give a brief example, consider the vague status code **LM** mentioned earlier. If a collector was given a new file to work at the beginning of a month, collecting small balance credit cards with an average balance of $500.00, and for the first week the collector left 100 voicemail messages. Out of the 100-voicemail messages the collector talked to 10 debtors and setup 5 payment arrangements, generating $2,500.00 for the week. From this view it would seem as though the collector is doing great, because at this rate, if the collector generates the same amount for the next 3 weeks in the month he/she will close out the month at $10,000.00. Now we will consider the same scenario, just from a different vantage point and ask just one question concerning effectiveness; **out of the 100 voicemail messages how many were direct attempts**, meaning the debtors identified themselves by name on the voicemail. This extremely important information, because without this information there is no way to know if the collector is delivering a strong effective message or a weak ineffective message. For instance, say that **GPD** (good phone number for debtor) was the status code used to describe when a collector left a message where the debtor's name was on the voicemail; and out of the 100 messages 30 were direct attempts, and the collector talked to only 10 debtors and closed 5. As you can see from this view, the collector missed 20 direct attempts and at $500.00 per account, (YEP!) a whopping $10,000.00 for one week lost due to ineffective message leaving. Now the $2,500.00 for the week that we celebrated before seems to be a problem, because the potential $10,000.00 for the month at the rate of $2,500.00 per week is small potatoes when compared to the potential $40,000.00 lost at the rate of $10,000.00 per week.

The File Management Tracker

At this point, you're probably asking yourself how can I see, find out and /or keep track of this exact information without wasting valuable time out of my workday, and my answer is the **File Management Tracker**. Exhibit A is a File Management Tracker, I developed this system of documentation to show the exact information needed to reveal strengths as well as weaknesses and give a detailed blue print of what happened on any given workday. At first glance this document may look simple, however it is extremely powerful. This system will give a clear picture of the most important information needed to effectively work a collection file and if used properly will increase your effectiveness as well as productivity by more than double. Using this very system I have hired, trained and developed individuals with no collections experience and within 30 to 45 days transformed them into the top performers.

How to use the File Management Tracker

As a collector there are questions that you have to ask yourself while working a collection file. To be truly effective and to put yourself in the best possible position to capitalize on each and every opportunity, you will have to know this information at the end of each day.

- How many good debtor numbers did I call, (debtor's name on the voicemail) and left a message on?
- How many debtors did I talk to?
- How many good third party numbers did I call, (third party's name on the voicemail) and left a message on?
- How many third parties did I talk to?
- How many visa promises did I get?
- How many payment promises did I get?

There are two sides to each bar. The right side is the **message side** of the bar, and the left is the **debtor contact side**.

TTD VP PMT _____Debtor's name_____ ___acct #___ GP GR GW PP PR TT3

Messages side of the tracker

GP: Good phone number for the debtor
GR: Good phone number for the reference

Good phone number for the debtor or third party means the debtor or third party name was on the voicemail. It is extremely important when working a file that you know exactly how many good numbers you called in a given day. Having this information will show you how effective your messages are.

TTD VP PMT _____Debtor's name_____ _____Account #_____ **(GP) (GR)** GW PP PR TT3

GW: Good work number for the debtor
This means the debtor currently works at the location you called. You will want to be careful when leaving messages on work phones. There could be multiple people listening to the debtor's voicemail and you may run the risk of third party disclosure.

TTD VP PMT _____Debtor's name_____ _____Account #_____ GP GR **(GW)** PP PR TT3

PP: Possible phone number for the debtor
PR: Possible phone number for the reference

Possible Phone for the debtor or third party means that the debtor's or third party name was not on the voicemail and a message was left. This is an area where many opportunities are lost. Most collectors will not leave a message on voicemail if there is no name attached. Understand, just because the debtor or third party name is not on the voicemail, doesn't mean the phone number does not belong to that debtor or third party. That being said, if a name is not attached you should leave the message anyway, just do not disclose information regarding a debt being collected. You have already dialed the number, it's a chance that it may be the debtor; if it's not, you stand to lose nothing.

TTD VP PMT _____Debtor's name_____ _____Account #_____ GP GR GW **(PP) (PR)** TT3

TT3: Talked to third party

It is important you understand that talking to a third party does not mean you simply talked to a third party and the person says he/she has not seen or heard from the debtor. Talking to a third party means that you gave a third party a message to deliver to the debtor. This is an important distinction because it reveals how effective you are at the Reference Relay. **You should never talk to a third party and not give a message to deliver**.

TTD VP PMT _____Debtor's name_____ _____Account #_____ GP GR GW PP PR **(TT3)**

Debtor Contact side of the tracker

TTD: Talk to debtor

Talked to debtor means that you actually talk to the person owing the debt, and delivered a Talk off.

(TTD) VP PMT _____Debtor's name_____   _____Account #_____   GP GR GW PP PR TT3

VP: Visa promise

Visa promise means that you talked to the debtor, delivered a Talk-off and the debtor did not have a bank account and promised to call back with a prepaid Visa or Master card.

TTD **(VP)** PMT _____Debtor's name_____   _____Account #_____   GP GR GW PP PR TT3

PMT: Payment Arrangement

Payment arrangement means the debtor provided banking information and gave a date the debt will be paid.

TTD VP **(PMT)** _____Debtor's name_____   _____Account #_____   GP GR GW PP PR TT3

Document messages not calls

When using the tracker, there are a couple of important things you must understand to unleash its power. First is understanding that the only people that will call you back are the people (debtor or third party) that you leave a message with; so it only makes sense to keep a record of each time you leave a message and where. At first thought, for the seasoned collector this may seem a little cumbersome, because they are under the impression that they leave hundreds of messages in a workday. However, after using this system after one day, collectors are always surprised as to how few messages they actually leave in a given workday. The reason this is often misinterpreted is because collectors have been **number of calls** driven and never really paid much attention to the amount of messages they leave. **Remember, voicemail messages are the force that drives your effectiveness.**

No double entries

Secondly, you must understand that there should be no double entries, meaning one bar will represent any action taken on any one account. For example, if you leave a message on a good number for the debtor and you leave a message on a possible number for the reference, you would not use a different bar. You would enter the debtor's name and account number once and circle GP and PR showing the two separate actions taken on one account using one bar. Moreover, if the debtor calls back the next day, you would simply return to the tracker from the previous day and circle the TTD disposition.

Never place third party's names on track

When using the tracker throughout your workday you should never use a third party name on the section for debtor's name. When a message is left for a third party, you will write the debtor's name and account number in the appropriate place and simply circle the disposition to indicate that a message will left for a third party GR or PR. (An example and explanation of how this process will help you with the Reference Relay is provided with Exhibit B)

To illustrate how to use the tracker appropriately I will use five bars, with an explanation for each.

1. **(TTD)** VP **(PMT)** _____John Doe_____ __0987431__ **(GP)** GR GW PP PR TT3

    As you can see on this bar that the collector called a good phone number for the debtor (name on the voicemail). Convinced the debtor to call in and delivered an effective Talk—off (the debtor provided banking information and a date for the payment).

2. **(TTD)** VP PMT ___Mary Jane___ ___0987432___ GP **(GR)** GW PP PR **(TT3)**

    As you can see on this bar that the collector called a good phone number for a third party (third party name on the voicemail). Delivered an effective Reference Relay, in turn convincing the debtor to call in. However didn't deliver an effective Talk-off.

3. **(TTD) (VP) (PMT)** ___Chris Good___ __0987433__ GP GR GW **(PP)** PR TT3

As you can see on this bar the collector called and left a message on possible phone number for the debtor (debtor did not identify him/herself on the voicemail), however it was in fact a good contact number. The collector delivered an effective Talk-off and the debtor didn't have a bank account, but the collector was able to convince the debtor to call back within 24 hours with a prepaid card, and an arrangement was set.

4. **(TTD) (VP)** PMT ____Sam Hill____ __0987434__ GP GR GW PP **(PR) (TT3)**

As you can see on this bar the collector called a possible number of a third party (third party did not identify him/herself on voicemail). The third party called in, the collector delivered an effective reference relay that convinced the debtor to call in. However, didn't deliver an effective Talk-off, because he/she didn't create enough urgency to have the debtor call back with a prepaid.

5. **(TTD)** VP **(PMT)**____Susie Cue____ __0987435__ GP GR **(GW)** PP PR TT3

As you can see on this bar the collector called a good work number for the debtor, the collector delivered an effective Talk-off and a payment arrangement was set.

Exhibit A
Date_____

File Management Tracker

Debtor Name   Acct#

TTD VP PMT_____ _____ GP GR GW PP PR TT3
TTD VP PMT_____ _____ GP GR GW PP PR TT3
TTD VP PMT_____ _____ GP GR GW PP PR TT3
TTD VP PMT_____ _____ GP GR GW PP PR TT3
TTD VP PMT_____ _____ GP GR GW PP PR TT3
TTD VP PMT_____ _____ GP GR GW PP PR TT3
TTD VP PMT_____ _____ GP GR GW PP PR TT3
TTD VP PMT_____ _____ GP GR GW PP PR TT3
TTD VP PMT_____ _____ GP GR GW PP PR TT3
TTD VP PMT_____ _____ GP GR GW PP PR TT3
TTD VP PMT_____ _____ GP GR GW PP PR TT3
TTD VP PMT_____ _____ GP GR GW PP PR TT3
TTD VP PMT_____ _____ GP GR GW PP PR TT3
TTD VP PMT_____ _____ GP GR GW PP PR TT3
TTD VP PMT_____ _____ GP GR GW PP PR TT3
TTD VP PMT_____ _____ GP GR GW PP PR TT3
TTD VP PMT_____ _____ GP GR GW PP PR TT3
TTD VP PMT_____ _____ GP GR GW PP PR TT3
TTD VP PMT_____ _____ GP GR GW PP PR TT3
TTD VP PMT_____ _____ GP GR GW PP PR TT3

Exhibit B

File Management Tracker

	Debtor Name	Acct#
(TTD) VP **(PMT)**	<u>Amy Dye</u>	<u>123456</u> **(GP)** GR GW PP PR TT3
TTD VP PMT	<u>Sam Hill</u>	<u>234345</u> GP**(GR)** GW PP PR **(TT3)**
(TTD) VP **(PMT)**	<u>Susie Cue</u>	<u>674638</u> GP GR GW **(PP)** PR TT3
TTD VP PMT	<u>John Doe</u>	<u>573845</u> GP GR GW PP **(PR)** **(TT3)**
(TTD) (VP) (PMT)	<u>Al Good</u>	<u>574638</u> GP GR **(GW)** PP PR TT3
TTD VP PMT	<u>Mary Jane</u>	<u>392747</u> GP GR GW **(PP)** PR TT3
TTD VP PMT	<u>Stew Best</u>	<u>874646</u> GP GR GW PP **(PR)** TT3
TTD VP PMT	<u>Rhonda Help</u>	<u>937567</u> GP **(GR)** GW PP PR **(TT3)**
(TTD) VP PMT	<u>Billy Jean</u>	<u>457859</u> **(GP)** GR GW PP PR TT3
TTD VP PMT	<u>Jamie Bonds</u>	<u>094374</u> GP GR GW (PP) PR TT3
TTD VP PMT	<u>Johnie Han</u>	<u>637648</u> GP **(GR)** GW PP PR **(TT3)**
(TTD) (VP) PMT	<u>Greg Lottery</u>	<u>843285</u> GP GR GW **(PP)** PR TT3
TTD VP PMT	<u>Mitch Hamer</u>	<u>765849</u> GP GR GW PP **(PR)** **(TT3)**
(TTD) VP **(PMT)**	<u>Sue What</u>	<u>764845</u> **(GP)** GR GW PP PR TT3
TTD VP PMT	<u>Mel Man</u>	<u>139578</u> GP **(GR)** GW **(PP)** (PR) TT3
(TTD) VP **(PMT)**	<u>Hein Duncan</u>	<u>564356</u> GP GR **(GW)** PP PR TT3
TTD VP PMT	<u>Fret Loops</u>	<u>455324</u> GP GR GW PP **(PR)** **(TT3)**
TTD VP PMT	<u>Blue Fox</u>	<u>883246</u> GP **(GR)** GW PP PR **(TT3)**
(TTD) VP **(PMT)**	<u>Trey Muzic</u>	<u>643567</u> GP **(GR)** GW **(PP)** PR **(TT3)**

Exhibit B shows a completed tracker, as you are able to see clearly, this collector has an excellent Talk-off (closing on 6 out of 8 opportunities), a powerful voicemail message for both third parties and debtors; (every message left where a name was on the voicemail, the collector received a call back) however, the collector struggles with the Reference Relay. Out of 8 attempts the collector only had one successful Reference Relay. Notice, in just one day of work the collector missed seven opportunities. Now, consider for a moment if each of these missed opportunities were $800.00. Although the collector will potentially generate $4,800.00 the collector cost this agency another $5,600.00 in potential earning due to one deficiency in the 5 elements.

Debtor call back scenario using the tracker

To explain how you will use the tracker through out your day, week, or month say that Mary Jane called in from bar 6. As you can see the collector left a message where there was no name present on the voicemail. If Mary Jane calls in, the collector would follow the Talk-off structure by asking the debtor's name and then place the debtor on hold. The collector would then survey the tracker find the debtor's name, pull the account information and set up for Talk off delivery.

Third party call back: Reference Relay Scenario using the Tracker

Bar 14 debtor (Mel Man) shows two messages were left for third parties, one with the name on the voicemail and one without. It's important to understand that you should never place the third parties name on the tracker, only the debtor's name and account number. Remember with the Third parties message we left both names on the voicemail, now if the third party calls in when he or she states their name, you would place them on hold. When you survey the tracker you will notice that the name given is not present, so immediately you know it's a third party. You return to the call and ask, *"was it another name associated with the voicemail"*, the third party will say *"yes, Mel Man"*. You would then place the third party on hold for a second time and pull Mel's account and set up for Reference Relay delivery.

Conclusion

Although a career in the collection industry can be quite rewarding if you understand and follow the core principles provided in this book; the one key characteristic that is essential to becoming a top performer in any profession is hunger. **A person can be taught what to say and how to say it, however a person cannot be taught hunger.** You have to want to be the best and capitalize on every opportunity, no matter your chosen profession.

Debt Terms

Account condition: shows the present state of the account, however does not indicate the payment history of the account that led to the current state.

Account number: The unique number assigned by a creditor to identify a debtor's account with the creditor.

Accounts in Good Standing: Credit items that have a positive status.

Accounts Receivable: A business transaction or series of business transactions that manage the billing of customers who owe a debt.

Adjustment: Percentage of the debt that is to be repaid to the creditors in a Chapter 13 bankruptcy.

Aging Report of Schedule: A list of accounts receivable broken down by number of days until due or past due.

Annual fee: A special charge credit card issuers often requires a borrower to pay once a year, for the use of their service.

Annual Percentage Rate (APR): A measure of how much interest credit will cost.

Authorized User: Person permitted by a credit cardholder to charge goods and services on the cardholder's account but who is not responsible for repayment of the debt.

Bad debt: a fiscal amount of receivables that is considered unrecoverable.

Balloon payments: Requires a single, lump-sum payment be made at the end of the loan.

Bankrupt: Legally declares an inability to pay creditors.

Bankrupt code: Federal laws governing the condition and procedures under which persons claiming inability to repay their debts can seek relief.

Chapter 7 Bankruptcy: Is a chapter of the bankruptcy code that provides for the administered liquidation of the assets of a financially troubled individual or business.

Chapter 11 Bankruptcy: Is a chapter of the bankruptcy code used for the reorganization of financially trouble business. (An alternative to liquidation under Chapter 7.)

Chapter 12 Bankruptcy: Is a chapter of the bankruptcy code adopted to address the financial crisis of the farming community.

Chapter 13 Bankruptcy: Is a chapter of the bankruptcy code where debtors repay debts according to a plan accepted by the debtor, the creditors and the court. Plan payments are paid to creditors through the court system and the bankruptcy trustee.

Charge-off: Action of transferring accounts deemed uncollectible, the accounts are no longer considered part of a company's receivable or profit picture.

Civil Action: Any court action against a consumer to regain money for another party.

Claim amount: The amount awarded in a court action.

Closed Date: The date an account was closed.

Co-maker: A co-maker is legally responsible to repay debt in the joint account agreement.

Collection Agency: Is a business that charges a fee to collect debt.

Consumer Credit Counseling Service: Is a non-profit organization that assists consumers in dealing with their credit problems.

Co-signer: An individual who pledges in writing on a credit contract to repay the debt if the borrower fails to do so.

Credit Limit/Line of Credit: The maximum amount a borrower can draw from a open end credit.

Credit Items: information reported by creditors to the credit bureaus.

Credit Report: Is a confidential report on a consumer's payment history, reported by their creditor to the consumer credit reporting agencies.

Credit Score: A tool used by credit grantors to aid in determining risk in granting credit.

Creditor: Party that claims another party owes it some form of capital.

Creditworthiness: The ability of a consumer to receive favorable consideration for the use of credit from a lender.

Date Filed: The date a publish record was awarded.

Date status: On the credit report, date the creditor last reported information about the account.

Date Opened: The date on the credit report, indicating the date an account was opened.

Date Resolved: The completion date of a public record item.

Debtor: An individual or business that owes money to a creditor.

Delinquent: Accounts classified according to number of day past due, such as 30, 60, 90, and 120 days past due. Classifications also include charge-off, repossession, transferred, etc.

Disclosure: Provides the consumer with his or her credit history as required by the FCRA.

Dismissed: When a consumer files a bankruptcy, and the judge decides not allow the consumer to continue with the bankruptcy.

Dispute: When a consumer challenges an item on their credit report that he or she believe to be inaccurate or incomplete.

Dunning letter: A series of accounts receivable letters detailing the attempts made to collect on an unpaid debt. The letters usually serve as a legal requirement for debt collectors when attempting to collect unpaid debt.

ECOA: Standard abbreviation for Equal Credit Opportunity Act.

Equal Credit Opportunity Act (ECOA): Federal Law, which prohibits creditors from discriminating against credit applicants on the basis of sex, marital status, race, color, religion, age, and/or receipt of public assistances.

Equifax: A national credit-reporting agencies,(headquartered in Atlanta, Ga.) The other two are **Experian** and **TransUnion**.

Fair Credit and Charge Card Disclosure Act: Amendments to the Truth in Lending Act. This Act requires lenders to disclose all costs involved in credit card plans that are offered by mail, telephone or applications distributed to the general public.

Fair Credit Billing Act: A federal legislation that provides a specific error resolution procedure to protect credit card customers from making payments on inaccurate billing.

Fair Credit Reporting Act (FCRA): Federal legislation governing the action of credit reporting agencies.

Fair Debt Collection Practices Act (FDCPA): Federal legislation prohibiting abusive and unfair debt collection practices.

Finance charge: Amount of interest paid.

First party: An entity that is a subsidiary of the original creditor in a two party contract.

Fixed Rate: An annual percentage rate that does not change.

Grace Period: The time period debtor has to pay a bill in full to avoid interest charges.

Guarantor: An individual responsible for paying a bill.

Installment Credit: Credit accounts where debt is divided into specific amount to be paid at specified intervals.

Judgment Granted: A final determination of the rights of the parties involved in a lawsuit.

Last reported: The date the creditor last reported information about the account.

Liability amount: An amount a debtor is legally obligated to pay by a creditor.

Lien: Legal document used to create a security interest in a debtor property. For example, a lien can be placed against a consumer property for failure to pay the city, county, state or federal government money that is owed, meaning the consumer's property is being used as collateral during repayment period.

Obsolescence: A term used to describe how long negative information will stay in a credit file before it is deemed relevant in a credit granting decision.

Original Amount: The original amount owed to a creditor.

Payment Status: Reflects the history of the account, show any delinquencies or derogatory conditions occurring during the previous seven years.

Petition: If a consumer files a bankruptcy, but a judge has not yet ruled that it can proceed, it is known as bankruptcy petitioned.

Plaintiff: an individual that initially brings legal action against another (defendant) seeking a court decision.

Potentially Negative Items: Any potentially negative credit items of public records that may have as effect on your creditworthiness.

Public Record Data: information on a credit report, that is limited to tax liens, lawsuits and judgments that relate to the consumer's debt obligations.

Recent Balance: The most recent balance owed on an account as reported by the creditor.

Recent Payment: The most recent amount paid on an account as reported by the creditor.

Released: a lien has been satisfied in full.

Repossession: A creditor taking possession of property pledge as collateral on a loan contract.

Satisfied: When a consumer has paid all of the money the court determines he or she owes, the public record item is satisfied.

Secured Credit: Loan for which some form of collateral, has been pledges for the term of a loan.

Settle: An agreement between the debtor and the lender where the debtor repays only part of the original debt.

Terms: This refers to the debt repayment terms of an agreement with a creditor.

Third-Party Collectors: Collection agents who are under contract to collect debts for a collection agency.

Truth in Lending Act: Title I of the Consumer Protection Act. Requires that most categories of lender disclose the annual interest rate, the total dollar cost and other term of loans and credit sales.

Unsecured Credit: Credit for which no collateral has been pledged.

Usury: Charging an illegally high interest rate on a loan.

Vacated: Indicates a judgment that was rendered void or set aside.

Variable Rate: An annual percentage rate that may change over time as the prime-lending rate varies of according to the terms of contract with the lender.

Voluntary Bankruptcy: When a consumer files the bankruptcy on his own.

Wage assignment: A signed agreement by a consumer, permitting a creditor to collect a certain portion of the debtor's wages from an employer in the event of default.

Writ of Replevin: A legal document issued by a court authorizing repossession of security.

Reference

Wikipedia